Nobody Asked Me But...

It Isn't Easy Being Jewish

This is the kind of book everybody should have. It's perfect for reading while you wait to pick up the kids or while your wife is shopping. It's a great book to take to the bathroom.

Stan Cohen is a wonderful story teller and he reveals himself in bits and pieces as he moves from one story to another. There are childhood stories, stories of a young man facing adulthood in the army and later in the hospital. There are stories of marriage and life and all of them bring a smile or a tear and sometimes both at the same time.

Each story should be consumed at one time. They're poignant—as a little boy delivers telegrams during World War II or when Stan faces brain surgery for cancer at the age of 28. There are stories about his job with the Internal Revenue Service and an absolutely hysterical story about a "male surgical procedure."

These stories are wistful, funny and often insightful. Stan Cohen says it isn't easy being Jewish, but he sure makes it entertaining!

Phil Johnston, PhD.
Fountain Valley, CA

Nobody asked me but...
It isn't easy being Jewish

Stan Cohen

ISBN 1-932252-77-0

First Edition   10 9 8 7 6 5 4 3 2

Published by

Creative Continuum, Inc.
2910 E. La Palma Ave., Suite C
Anaheim, CA 92806
714-630-2960
www.creativecontinuum.com

CONTENTS

Dedication

Over my wife Pat's objections, I am dedicating this book to her.

I've loved two women in my life, my mother and Pat. My mother lived to 95; but Pat, my cancer-stricken wife of 40 plus years, has been everything to me. Pat passed away onFebruary 16, 2007. In her own way, she taught me that being Catholic is not bad at all. Pat taught me to appreciate most Catholic believers and not to question their beliefs. In her own way, she has been and was criticizing the Church without saying so out loud.

She took me to every Church she could, both in Orange County and the world. We even visited one, the Notre Dame Basilica in Montreal, Canada that charged $4 admission just to look around.

To our surprise, because we are of different faiths, our marriage lasted 40 years because we refrained from discussing the points that the Church itself questions. For example: the place of women in the Church, abortion, the death penalty, illegal immigrants, and so forth.

So, I owe everything to my best pal, my wife, Pat. When Pat got to Heaven and met God, I believe He said, "Pat, thanks be to Me, you're here! Now we can get this place organized!"

What A Day

The water was warm. Getting out of a warm bed on a cold morning into a warm bath was nice.

"Mom, can you bring the radio into the bathroom so I can listen to Ray Block's Make Believe Ballroom?"

"No, no!!! You know you can't take a bath with electricity in the bathroom!!!" she reminded me.

It was a cold, October 1941 morning about 8:30. "Mom, why do I have to take a bath on Saturday? Sunday night, before school on Monday, is supposed to be my time."

"Would you lower your voice," she countered, "you'll wake your brother."

So what, I thought. If I'm up, he should be.

We Cohens lived in a very small, two bedroom, three family house in the heart of Flatbush, near Ebbets Field, the home of my favorites, the Brooklyn Dodgers. I was 8 and ½ years old (the ½ year was very important because I was that much closer to running away from home) and had to sleep with my 13-year-old brother, Eddie.

It was my turn to sleep next to the one window in the room I shared with my brother. Eddie always managed to sleep by the window in the summer; I was stuck with the window in the snowy winter.

Pop was at work at the cafeteria, making food for the few folks who also had to work on Saturdays.

"I'm not letting you leave this house, travel alone on the subway, and visit my sister (Aunt Helen was always referred to as Mom's sister, not my aunt) with that filthy body of yours. Make sure you wash those potato filled ears!!!" Every time that I had to take a bath, once per week or on special occasions, Mom would say I had enough dirt in my ears to grow potatoes.

"Mom, why do I have to visit your sister? Is she going to holler at me because you had to come to school to get me out of the principal's office?" I got in trouble in school this time for going to the Dodger ballgame for the "umpteenth" time during school hours.

"Keep quiet! And make sure you wash those ears! If not, I'll come in there and help you!"

"No, no," I quickly responded. "Don't come in here!!!" I was modest and anyway, I was too old to have a female looking at my naked body.

Why did my Aunt Helen call so early today and insist she wanted to speak with me privately? I had five other aunts from my father's family but my Aunt Helen, my mom's only sister, was different. She was very tall, well educated and made a zillion dollars as the showman Billy Rose's private secretary. She was the only aunt I feared.

Boy, I must be in real trouble. Mom was allowing me, for the first time, to travel alone on the subway. I must remember to watch for kidnappers, drunks and holdup men and go into other subway cars if I see any. I wondered how they would look.

I just knew my visit to Aunt Helen's was going to be terrible. Mom had laid out THE suit containing long pants. The only other time I wore this suit was at my brother's Bar Mitzvah last March. All my other pants were either shorts or knickers with long sox to keep my legs warm.

I finished washing, of course skipping that area that good men didn't touch, and doing my ears twice. I quickly dried myself, wrapping the wet towel around me. The bedroom was cold and Eddie began to stir.

"Where are you going so early on a Saturday?" he mumbled.

"None of your business," I mumbled back and continued to dress. Let him guess.

"Would you please hurry," Mom said from the kitchen, "You

can't keep my sister waiting!" Mom gave away my secret.

"You're going to see Aunt Helen?" Eddie said. "Boy are you in trouble! And you're going to miss my championship softball game at the waterworks." The waterworks was a dirt field two blocks away where all the kids played every kind of sport. No parks! I was looking forward to seeing Eddie play but when Aunt Helen called, everyone responded.

I quickly dressed, having Mom tie my brother's Bar Mitzvah tie around my neck. Gulping down my fresh squeezed orange juice with a half of yesterday's donut, I kissed my mom. She reminded me about the kidnappers, checked my tie and pushed me out the door.

"Do you remember how to get to my sister's?" she shouted to me.

"Oh Mom, stop worrying! I have been on the subway a zillion times." I tried to remember the station I was to get off at. It was ten o'clock.

I walked the two short blocks to the elevated BMT, Brighton Beach Line, waited a few minutes for the train to arrive and boarded. The ride was uneventful (no kidnappers) and arrived at Aunt Helen's "stop" about 45 minutes later. I came out of the subway and walked to Aunt Helen's apartment house.

The apartment house on 10th Street in the Greenwich Village section of Manhattan was tremendous with about a zillion apartments. The entire house was guarded by an imposing black man, known by my aunt as "The Black Doorman". He called Aunt Helen and told her of my arrival. I was escorted by him to the elevator. I was too nervous to tell him I knew where the elevator was. As I stepped in to the elevator, he reached over and pressed the "5" button. After the door closed, the elevator began moving.

My Aunt Helen was standing at her door, waiting for the elevator to arrive. She was an imposing figure and beautiful. She and Uncle Ike had no children of their own so they "adopted"

Aunt Helen and Uncle Ike, about 1945

my brother and I as their own. Even though I felt a little uncomfortable in their presence, I deeply loved and admired them both. Deep down, I wished I had grown up to be like them.

"You're late! Don't take off your coat; we are immediately leaving for lunch." she said.

"Where's Uncle Ike?" I said.

"He's doing a little work at his office today. I thought just you and I could spend the day together, just talking."

"Uh oh, I'm in trouble," I thought.

"Where would you like to go to lunch?" she asked.

"My favorite!" I answered. "The Jewish Deli."

"Done," she said.

Aunt Helen ordered a taxicab from "The Black Doorman".

The taxi was waiting in front of her apartment house when we came down. It sped off as she said, "The Second Avenue Delicatessen, please."

We talked about Mom and Pop but arrived at the Deli before getting around to my brother. As we walked in, a man behind the counter greeted her. "Hello, Helen! Who's the nice young man with you?"

"My favorite nephew, Stanley," she replied. (I hated that name.)

A table with a very large menu was our next stop. It had a zillion items. I ordered my favorite, a corned beef sandwich with a Coca-Cola. My aunt ordered only a cup of coffee and lit a cigarette. She knew I wouldn't be able to finish that large sandwich so she took half. The whole sandwich was just enough for both of us.

We talked of Eddie and my school but nothing of Mom coming to "bail" me out of the principal's office. So far so good. My Aunt Helen spoke of Uncle Ike and had a constant smile on her face and in her voice. Maybe, just maybe, I hoped.

"Have you had enough," she said as she pulled some bills out of her purse, "...or would you like dessert?"

"No, no," I said, "I'm full."

"Come on, it's 12:30, just enough time to get to the theater." she said, getting into a cab.

Theater? What theater, I thought. What was my Aunt Helen up to? As the cab sped towards the theatrical district uptown, my mind and heart raced. Was my loving aunt treating me to my first show? Was I going to the theater with my Aunt Helen and seeing my very first Broadway show? Oh, I hope. I said nothing, holding my breath.

And, as we rounded the corner, there it was!!! The marquee with "Finnian's Rainbow" in large letters and pictures of the stars on it. Was I excited!

Aunt Helen paid the cab and rushed me into the theater. We sat in the "House Seats," fourth row center in the orchestra.

For the next three hours my mouth didn't close. I sat quietly, applauding gently when appropriate and changed my contemplated professions many times. It was glorious.

As we left the theater, my Aunt said, "Well, how did you like the show?"

I replied, "Oh, it was terrific!!! Thank you so very much for taking me."

The rest of the day went by in a blur. Uncle Ike coming home to Aunt Helen; Mom, Pop and Eddie arriving at Helen and Ike's to take me home; the forty-five minute drive; undressing and getting into my bed next to the cold window;

Mom saying, "...and did my sister ball you out today?" as she put me to bed.

"Nope!" I answered, smiling.

How clearly I remember those dreams that night.

Memories of WWII

CHAPTER TWO

Mom, me at 11, and Pop in 1944

The lady was retreating back into her house and repeating over and over again, "No...no...no," as she slammed the door in my face.

It was 1944 and I was eleven and had my very first job at Western Union, delivering telegrams from the home office to people's homes in my neighborhood. I worked Thursday afternoons after school and Saturday mornings, before playing football with my friends. It those days, people did not give delivery boys tips, but the 15 cents an hour pay helped a little at home. At least it paid for my movies.

It was fun riding my old bike from the Western Union Office on Kings Highway to the houses in Flatbush. I knew the streets in the area, and the fresh air, especially in the cold winter, was exhilarating. However, my first job and the 15 cents an hour didn't matter much when I had to deliver "those" telegrams. Most of "those" telegrams were telling moms and dads that their sons were killed in the war. That part was no fun.

Going to peo-

> I was too young to serve in the Armed Forces during World War II, but like any war, it left a lasting impression.

ple's homes, seeing the looks on their faces, hearing them shout, cry, and shake all over were sights and sounds I will never forget. I never became immune to those feelings and I quickly realized how death was so permanent. And here was I, a boy of eleven, telling friends and neighbors news that would change their lives forever. It wasn't a fun job after all.

And then it happened. The Sarokin family, two blocks from my home, were to receive a telegram from the War Department that their son, George, had been killed in the "Battle of the Bulge." The Saturday before, I had played football with his younger brother, Billy.

I watched mesmerized as the Western Union Operator received the message on the yellow ticker tape, tore the tape to its proper length and pasted the sentences on the standard yellow paper. "We regret to inform you that your son, George Sarokin, was killed during action in Bastogne, Germany on December 21, 1944. Further details will follow." The operator sealed the message and handed it to me to deliver. Oh, my God!

Slowly peddling my bike, I made my way to the house in our neighborhood. Walking up the steps to the porch, I gently knocked at the door. Mrs. Sarokin greeted me in her usual cheery fashion. "Hi Stanley, Billy is not here." I could not speak. I was too emotional. Without saying a word, I reached into the back pocket of my knickers, and handed her the yellow envelope. Mrs. Sarokin looked at me, then at the envelope. Without opening the envelope, her smile turned to tears. She knew what it said. Then reluctantly, she read it and said, "Thank you, Stanley. I'll tell Billy you were here."

Mrs. Sarokin slowly turned and gently closed the door. I quit my job the following Thursday.

Water, water everywhere

As a boy, I lived two blocks from Ebbets Field, home of the crazy Brooklyn Dodgers. At that time there was no television or night games, so as their number one fan, I needed to play "hooky" from school whenever there was a home game. On this day in May, I was standing on Bedford Avenue only about twenty-five feet outside the stadium, staring at a one hundred foot wall.

I was standing there, with my baseball mitt, hoping against hope that someone, anyone would hit a ball over the wall so I could catch the ball and go home that night with a precious souvenir. I couldn't afford the 25 cents it cost to sit in the bleachers.

That day—a school day for everyone else but me—it was hot. Very HOT! I stood there, my Dodger cap getting a white ring on its sweatband, pounding my glove. Nothing, nothing but cheers. No home runs in my direction.

I looked all around my waiting spot on Bedford Avenue and noticed a Catholic Church behind me with its doors open. The sun was unmerciful and I thought I would at least get out of the burning sun by standing in the doorway, out of the sunlight. Climbing the stairs, I entered the church. At least I was shaded from the scorching sun.

Looking around, I noticed a big bowl with liquid in it in the center of the entrance to the Church. I went to this bowl, sampled the liquid and discovered it was water and cool. I put my fingers in the receptacle and sampled the water. It was great! Noticing I was alone, I washed my hands and face in the water and drank quite a bit.

> This story tells about my "conversion to a Catholic" when I was only twelve.

As I was told sixty years later, it was "holy water," blessed by the presiding priest and used by the parishioners to "make the sign of the cross" before and after their worship services. So I found out I may have been "baptized" by the holy water. I thought I was a Catholic from that day on. My wife just laughed when I told her that!

Snow

Boy, was it COLD! It was a Saturday morning in December 1947 and it was snowing.

Our little apartment in the heart of Flatbush, Brooklyn was warm because my father had just stoked the basement furnace. Stoke meant to shake down the old, burnt coke in the grating and put new coke, or processed coal, into the furnace that heated the house. We got several dollars off our weekly—yes, I said weekly—rent for doing that little service. And it continued to snow!

My brother, Eddie, nineteen, who was attending City College of New York (CCNY), my mom and pop and me, who attended James Madison High School, lived directly across Avenue "R" from our Temple and Synagogue. We weren't a religious family but my brother and I attended Hebrew School until we were both Bar Mitzvah'ed at thirteen and attended the High Holy Days—Rosh Hashanah and Yom Kippur— (naturally, for a fee, you know the Jews) every year and occasionally tried to attend Sabbath or Friday and/or Saturday services. Still the snow came down.

For some reason or other, my father felt an obligation to clean the Temple's front walk and steps during such happenings. No one, not even Rabbi Steinbach or the "big wheels" at the Temple, had asked him to clean up after a heavy snowfall, but my father felt obliged. Being Saturday, of course there was no school and my father had decided not to open the Cafeteria in Manhattan because of what was happening outside. It was still snowing.

Mom said, "Boys, wear your boots and yocks over your sweaters!" "Yocks" was a term the Cohen family used to designate a very heavy coat. How were we going to shovel when the three of us were clothed like statues? "Stanley," I hated that name, "don't forget to wear your mufflers, both inside your jacket and outside."

"Yes, Mom." Why did women get out of this hard work? Why wasn't I born a girl?

The snow was getting serious. I guessed at least ten inches had already fallen by sundown. Us three men (oh, how I liked that phrase) walked out of our front door and into the snow. Pop started on the stairs into the Synagogue proper while Eddie was attempting to clean the sidewalk surrounding the School. My "assignment" was to follow them pushing the heavy piles into the street.

It continued snowing. It was like "shoveling against the tide." The more we shoveled, the heavier it came down. Us three were losing the battle. Pop finally said, "Let's call it quits." We did, shook ourselves off at the front door, left the wet clothes outside and entered the warm house.

We worked for hours, forty-five minutes if you trusted clocks. We three went to the front door, but Mom wouldn't let us in the house full of snow. She handed Pop and Eddie a hot cup of coffee. Me, she gave a glass of milk. Sure, they're warmed by the hot stuff while me... Mom always said coffee would stunt my growth. I was 5'8" and over 200 lbs. in high school. Cold milk!

The next morning dawned clear and bright. I looked out my window and gazed at twenty-seven inches of snow, a record for New York. The sun shone brightly on our Temple and the Cohen's. I thanked God, I didn't have to go to school that day!

The Day

The alarm clock rang to tell me it was 4:00AM. I hadn't slept all night. I was being drafted in the U.S. Army this morning.

I jumped out of my warm bed into a cold room. It was April 20, 1952, but the winter's chill still lingered in Brooklyn. My brother, Eddie, still sleeping in the same room whispered, "Would you keep quiet; I'm still sleeping." I guess he hadn't slept much either.

I went into the hall to wake my father in case he hadn't heard the alarm. He had and was in the bathroom already. My mom was stirring. It was chilly in our small apartment. Pop needs to shake down the burnt coals and re-stoke the furnace in the basement, I thought.

I waited a few minutes for Pop to emerge from the one bathroom so I could complete packing my bag with my few toilet articles. I made such a big deal out of buying a new razor and shaving cream for myself, because I used to use my brother's shaving stuff, and only once a week at that.

Completing my chores, I went into my room and turned on the dim light to help me dress. This time, Eddie yelled at me, "Would you be quiet!" Yeah, he'll really miss me, I thought.

I quickly dressed and

> In 1952, when my brother Eddie came home from his service during the Korean War, I received my draft notice. Soon I was to exchange my $200 a month job for a $52 a day, once a month job, with the Army. I remember the day that Pop took me to the Selective Service Office to report in.

with my small bag, went to the kitchen. Mom in her wool robe and Pop in his work clothes were sipping their hot coffee and orange juice and reading the morning's newspapers. It was 4:30. "Hurry up," Mom said, "You don't want to make your father late for work, do you?" Her eyes were red and swollen. She had been crying.

I had my milk and a half of a bagel. "I'll warm the car," Pop said calmly. He looked normal; my wonderful Pop who was respected by all of us.

I glanced at the newspapers. I couldn't look at Mom. I was afraid I would cry also. I had never been away from home before for any length of time, let alone going to Korea to be shot at. I was scared!

Pop came back to the apartment. "It's 4:45. Let's go." He was going to drop me off at the recruitment building in Manhattan and then continue on to 36th Street to open his cafeteria. It was time to go.

"Say good-bye to your brother," Mom said.

Eddie was five years older, had served his two years in the Navy and was finishing up college at City College of New York. I went into our bedroom and leaned down to hug him. He reached up with his arms, pulled me down to him and kissing me on the cheek, whispered, "I'll miss you...keep safe."

Then I really cried.

Rushing out of the bedroom, I almost fell into my mother's arms. "God protect you and keep you safe. Come home to me soon." She cried. I couldn't speak.

Grabbing my bag, I stumbled out of the apartment and into Pop's Buick. "I think I'm getting a little cold." I took my handkerchief out to blow my nose and wipe my eyes.

"I understand." Pop said.

The drive to Center Street in Manhattan was uneventful. There was little traffic. The only time Pop and I talked was when I admitted to him that I was scared. Again he said, "I understand."

As we approached the recruitment building, the traffic increased. It seemed like many people were dropping off their sons who had enlisted or been drafted and were reporting in. Pop stopped right in front of the building. Leaning over to me, he said, "gotta move." He kissed me flush on the lips and said, "God be with you." Then he practically pushed me out of the car and drove away.

Here I was, alone, standing in front of a big building, a new day was starting, along with a new chapter in my life. I was scared.

I was inducted at Fort Dix, New Jersey and bussed off to basic training at Aberdeen Proving Ground in Maryland, followed by six months in Texarkana, Texas for Advanced Infantry Training. The Army wanted to be certain that I was well-trained to be killed!

The Army's Basic Training and Me

Here are a few random thoughts on my first few months in the Army. When I was first drafted in April, the Army started the slow process of trying to make me into a "killing machine."

I spent the first week in Fort Dix, New Jersey where the Army gave me a uniform, a rifle and various other equipment and accessories. I spent the first week crying into my pillow at night because I was homesick and frightened.

One incident I will remember occurred after I just received my "dress uniform" from the Quartermaster at a hut in Fort Dix. First I received a very large duffle bag, which I was instructed to fill with any "civvies" (civilian clothes) I had brought with me from home. Someone said it was easier to burn them. Then the Army began to clothe me with the "right" clothes. I received two shoes of different sizes, shirts that were much too small for my 205-pound, 5-foot 11-inch frame, oversize pants that were much too long and wide and finally a "class A" hat which came down over my ears. When I complained that I could not see because the hat covered my eyes, the Quartermaster sergeant kept saying, "Don't worry, you'll grow into them!" What a mess.

As I left the quartermaster hut, I was handed a gun that was so dirty and covered with grease that again I complained. The sergeant said, "First of all, it's a rifle, don't let me ever here you call it a gun." As he held the rifle, he said, "...this is my rifle, this is my gun, (he grabbed his crotch), this is for fighting, this is for fun!" He continued, "Your job will be to clean that weapon. It will be defending you in combat."

I left the hut with my hands full and trying to look over the brim of my hat. The hike back to my barracks was across the open training field a few hundred yards away. As another soldier began to pass me I noticed he was impeccably dressed and had several ribbons on his chest. As he passed me, he stopped and said, "Soldier, don't you notice what's on my shoulders?" He pointed to a couple of shiny bars.

In response, I said, "What are you complaining about. Look what they gave me!"

After New Jersey, I was sent to Aberdeen Proving Grounds in Maryland. It was so big and took up so many miles, it WAS Maryland. I had ten weeks of basic training where I learned everything from first aid to weather reporting. One day, I found a cheap pair of glasses in the PX and wore them to our early morning inspection. I complained again to our sergeant that without my glasses, which I had to wear continually, I could not see the enemy. He said matter-of-factually, "Don't worry! We'll put you way up front! You won't miss a thing!"

In my letters to the family, I complained about always being hungry. My father, who worked at a Jewish delicatessen, sent me a two pound salami that could last until eaten. In my next letter, I told Pop that my Sergeant was always inspecting my backpack for unnecessary items. He would surely spot the salami. My father wrote back and said that I should strap it to my leg. I did. I walked funny and the aroma from my pants was something.

When I retuned from a week of leave at home, I was to report to Red River Arsenal in Texarkana, Texas. My mother tried to dutifully wash and iron my entire duffle bag. The family fed me to get me back to my original weight. In twelve weeks away from that "Jew food," I had lost almost fifty pounds and as the Sergeant had said, grew into almost everything.

Again, after many tearful goodbyes, I was on my way to Texas to Advanced Basic Training with no guarantee I would ever return. I guess a soldier needs advanced training to kill and/or be killed.

While in Texas I was subjected to many "whites only" signs and defied most of them. I was "sentenced" to KP (kitchen police) more than the average trainee because of my feelings for my black friends. While on KP, I developed heartburn so badly and of such duration that I thought I was born with it. One morning, when I awoke without the pain from heartburn, I went to "sick-call."

After ten weeks of Advanced Training where I learned how to fire a Browning Automatic Rifle (BAR) and drive and be rescued by a tank, I was sent home for a final time to wailing and worry from the family. Now, only occasionally, I cried into my pillow.

It was December and I reported to Fort Lewis in Seattle, Washington for my sea voyage to Korea. About two thousand of us waited and waited for our "ship to come in." Then it was time. For a change, it was pouring rain in Seattle that day and a troop train took us to the docks. Instead of loading the two thousand men on the ship immediately, the powers that be made us stand in the rain along side the ship. Then we heard a bell and saw a cart with three old ladies serving coffee to as many boys as they could. We were soaked but couldn't wait for their arrival. When the Red Cross wagon came to me, I asked politely for a coffee and a doughnut. When I was handed them, one of the women asked for 25 cents. I was completely floored. I said, "We are going to Korea to be shot at and probably killed and you want twenty-five cents from us? Shame on you!"

"Those are our orders," she responded. I have never contributed one penny to the Red Cross since that incident almost fifty-five years ago.

Then, it was on to Korea nineteen days away. I started to turn my head into the pillow again.

Korea Remembered

I vaguely remember my brother's admonition, "...don't volunteer for anything in the Army!" I thought for a moment. This sounded like a good job. I raised my hand.

It was raining and misting off and on as we disembarked from the *USS Sultan*, an Army Troop ship, in the bay at Inchon, Korea. The old hulk had transported the 1,250 of us for nineteen days from Seattle to Korea and had arrived on my twentieth birthday, February 10, 1953. The landing craft was rolling and shifting and with the rain and my clumsiness, I mostly slipped down the webbing into the boat. When the little boat had about twenty-five men, we headed for shore about a mile away.

Peering out from the silent boat, Korea looked foreboding. The low clouds, the mist, the flat hills devoid of any growth, the occasional distant rumble of cannon fire, I was both frightened and cocky. I had decided on the ship that I was being sent here to die; I was scared. And yet I had to continue to put up a "so what do I care" front to my buddies. We all acted the same. I'll bet the men around me were also crying inside.

It took about twenty minutes to cross the bay and unload our duffle bags and rifles in the landing areas. The rain was really coming down hard now; what a "Welcome to Korea!" this picture was. There were at least five hundred men in dripping helmets, ponchos to their ankles, rifles turned upside down to keep them dry, and rain seeping into their duffle bags. The Army, bah!!! How did they expect us to stay dry?

We all lined up in ranks the best we could. Soldiers scurrying about, tanks, trucks and jeeps all added to the mass confusion. An unknown Sergeant approached the assembled men and shouted, "No smoking. There's ammo here!!!" If he hadn't said anything, I wouldn't have missed a cigarette. Now I did.

"Sarge," I shouted, "how long you goin' to keep us standing here in the pouring rain?" He turned, glared at me and continued to walk away. My cockiness was showing.

Rain was dripping from my helmet. My face was wet. My poncho was soaked. I hoped I had packed my duffle bag well enough to keep the contents dry. My boots and my socks were wet. Lousy Army! They guaranteed the boots were waterproof. Baloney!

After about ten minutes, the sergeant returned and said, "See those 'Six-bys' over there? I need truck drivers." He pointed to the twenty or so big, ten wheel trucks standing vacant with what appeared to be dry cabs. "Any Transportation men in this group who would like to drive these vehicles into Seoul about fifty miles away? It will take all day; we will get you back to your outfits tonight."

Even though I had never driven anything larger than my father's Buick and that for less than two years, I raised my hand. You're right. I was being cocky again. The sergeant picked me!

About twenty-five of us ambled over to the trucks. I mean, these trucks were big! I got nervous. What would happen to me if I couldn't drive the truck? I didn't even know how to start it!

The men formed a circle. An important looking corporal said, "OK men. Pick out any truck, one driver to each. We will be heading down that dirt road directly to Seoul. Follow the man and his truck in front of you. Do what he does. Remember, no smoking in the cabs. We will give you plenty of breaks. Any questions?" None. "OK men, pick out a truck and let's roll 'em." I thought of a movie I'd seen.

I jumped into the truck with bright red flags on the front bumpers. The cab was very high but I managed to get my rifle and duffle bag on to the seat next to me. What a maze of levers, floor gearshifts, instructions and dials. I was at least twice as high as the men standing in the ranks I just left. The poor guys! As I was watching them, they began to march off down the road we were about to drive on. The rain was still falling but lighter now.

I was awakened from my reverie by the truck in front of me starting. I smelled that awful combination of exhaust and gasoline. I panicked! I've got to get this thing started. I quickly tried to read all the writing on the driver's panel in front of me. I turned the lever that said, "START." The engine quickly turned over, the truck lunged forward about a foot and the engine died. I had forgotten to push in the clutch and/or take it out of gear. I quickly made those adjustments, turned the lever once more and the engine "kicked" in and started to purr. I was proud of myself.

Just then the Corporal came by in his jeep and yelled up to me, "Is everything OK?"

"Great," I answered. "Just checking out everything." It was then I noticed that the fool truck had no windows, just a little old canvas covering my head. I took off my helmet and immediately got rain in my face.

"Put on that pot, soldier!!!", the Corporal said. "You sure you know how to drive this thing?"

"No sweat," I responded, and put on my helmet.

"Be sure to follow the driver in front of you. Whatever he does, you do. Got it?" he added. I saluted over the roar of all the engines.

In seconds, the truck in front of me began to move. I tried to move forward but stalled the engine. I had shifted into "overdrive" by mistake. The truck behind me began to honk his horn. I credited my wet face and body to the rain, not to sweat from my nervousness. I re-started the motor, shifted into first and quickly caught up to the truck in front of me. Now all I have to do is steer this monster and shift to second.

Somehow, I did those things but it took some doing. We

were now rolling down the dirt road at about twenty miles an hour with my fellow troops from the Sultan walking in single file on either side of us. Suckers!!! Look at me. Riding in relative comfort, not walking in the mud, the rain had stopped by then. Again, I thought of my brother's warning. Boy, was he wrong this time.

Suddenly, the truck in front of me stopped and shut off his motor. I followed suit. We were just fifteen minutes into the trip. It was then I heard the wail of a siren probably coming from the corporal's jeep at the head of our truck convoy. I noticed the soldiers leaving the main road and scattering into the mud ditches along the side of the road. The driver in front of me jumped from his cab and rolled in the water and mud under his truck. I followed. I burned my fingers on the hot exhaust pipes under my cab. We waited for at least five minutes. Silence, except for the siren. Then it was quiet. Nice break, I thought.

I reached under my water-soaked poncho and pulled out a wet cigarette pack with a lighter. I put a soaked cigarette into my mouth and lit it. Even though wet, the first puff tasted glorious.

At that moment, a jeep rolled up behind me and an officer of some rank shouted, "Are you crazy soldier, put out that cigarette. Don't you know what those red flags mean on your bumpers?"

"Sure I do, Sir, just thought this was a break." I quickly put my butt out. I had no idea what those red flags meant. More cockiness.

"You're lucky you didn't blow up the whole convoy and the soldiers around you," he said. "You can't smoke while you're transporting ammo." The words rung in my ears and through my brain. Ammunition! Ammunition! Is in this truck I'm driving? Oh my God, was my brother right.

The officer streaked away; the soldiers returned to the road; the driver and truck in front of me began to move and

I, after many deep breaths and curses directed at myself, did the same.

After about an hour on the road, the soldiers had been left behind. It was still barren all around us, not even a Burma Shave sign. The rain had stopped and there was a faint glimmer of sun peeping through the clouds. Did Korea have the same sun as we had in Brooklyn? I even smelled the human manure mingled with the exhaust fumes. My truck wandered to the side of the road as my mind wandered. I jerked the steering wheel. Better steer this thing right, I thought. Ammo in the back!

The truck in front stopped; the driver rolled under the cab and I nonchalantly did the same. I heard the familiar wail of the siren but this time, no cigarette and no burns. I missed the big puddle and remained fairly dry... but not for long.

I heard an approaching roar, which I later found out was from a jet engine. I glanced out from under my truck and saw a lone jet plane making a big "u" dive with the truck convoy at its' apex. Stupidly, I kept watching the jet as it approached and, in a matter of seconds, it had completed its' run. I noticed a big red star on the side of the jet as it passed about a hundred feet above me.

And then this powerful brain of mine went to work. The big red star meant it was NOT friendly! There were about twenty-five enemy trucks alone on this dirt road with no one or nothing around. There were pretty red flags on the bumpers of these twenty-five trucks denoting that these trucks were carrying ammunition. The pilot made a command decision. He'll come back over the convoy. I glanced to my rear. Here he comes.

I scrambled under my cab again and stuck my face and half my body in that big puddle under my truck. I started crossing myself like a good Catholic and saying the Jewish blessing for the Sabbath Day wine (that's the only Jewish prayer I could remember at the moment.) Then I said the "Our Father" as I thought a good Protestant would do. I was going to cover all bases. The jet roar became louder.

The "red star" jet again passed about a hundred feet above my truck but this time he was sprinkling bullets to the left and right of me. The roar of the jet and the sound those bullets made hitting the ground will never be forgotten by me. Occasionally, I still hear that sound when I can't sleep at night and it's very, very quiet.

The jet left. Miraculously, he had managed to miss every truck and everyone in our convoy.

I attribute my wetness to the puddle under my cab but like most men, in feeling myself to check for damage or injuries, I grabbed my crotch. Even though that part remained outside the puddle, it was wet.

I vaguely remember my brother saying, "...while in the Army, don't volunteer for ANYTHING!" I thought a moment. I raised my hand. Jerk!!!

E-E-E... Boom!

CHAPTER EIGHT

This is the best way I can describe the sound of an enemy mortar being lobbed towards our position. If you don't hear the "boom" ...

When I was in Korea in the Spring of 1953, I was assigned to a patrol team of ten men that left the barracks at midnight one night and returned the following midnight for twenty-four hours of R & R (rest and recuperation.) We were on duty twenty-four hours and twenty-four hours off with nothing to do but lie in our bunks, rest, and think about home. At least that is what I thought about at my tender, innocent age!

On patrol, my "partner" and foxhole mate was Carl Johnson, a good Catholic from Hutchinson, Kansas. We had chosen each other because we had nothing in common: religion, looks (he was handsome.), money (I had none) or education (I hardly made it through high school without flunking out). We made these patrols every other day for almost a month before that fateful day.

It was raining and the Sergeant said, "Don't forget your ponchos" as we were leaving the barracks at midnight. "Ponchos," I thought, "...they do nothing but get you wetter."

We walked through the mud until we reached our splitting-up point and the five teams went their ways. Carl and I wandered a little forward and to the left and "staked our claim." We were to watch for enemy infiltrators and if we saw any, we were to shoot a flare gun to warn the other men and battalion back at the post. So far, for most of the twenty-four hours on patrol, it was quiet and uneventful. There was, however, that sound that became ever-so familiar. "E-E-E Boom." Again, the "Boom" was quite important. If you failed to hear the "boom," well, maybe you can guess. Many came close, we could tell by the loudness of the sounds, but we always heard the "boom."

That night Carl was in a jovial mood, talking about this girl and what she wore before he had "had" her. There was a constant "E-E-E Boom" a distance from us and we almost disregarded it as we dug our foxhole. Now you think the Army would have enough sense to put us in the same spot this night so we could use the same hole as last night. No-o, we had a different spot, so we had to dig again. Thank God, the ground was soft from the rain.

The conversation easily went from girls to Coney Island and then back to girls, to Kansas' wheat fields, back to girls, finally settling on our favorite topic, religion. And still the E-E-E Boom continued, a little closer this time.

I tried to emphasize the Jewish idea that there was only one God and He alone controlled the universe. Carl said that Jesus was the Son of God and Jesus also was God. I thought we were both coming to the realization that our two religions weren't that far apart. Carl asked me to explain the miracles that Jesus had performed; the changing of water to wine and the feeding of thousands by producing fish in Galilee. I couldn't explain those supposed miracles and told my friend I didn't believe them. The E-E-E Boom was still making us pause during our conversation.

Once again, our thoughts turned to girls but Carl interrupted my "daydreaming" by asking another question about Jesus, as if an afterthought. "Do you believe that there ever was a Jesus Christ?" Carl asked. I answered, "Of course I do. He was a great man, a great philosopher who convinced most of the people there was another way to believe. He was a Jew, remember?"

At that moment there was that familiar E-E-E, but this time without the boom. I remember a flash. The next thing I remember, I was looking up at a white ceiling with a woman, all in white, standing over me. At that moment I thought Carl must have been right when, in previous talks, he tried to convince me that there was a Heaven.

"Stanley, Stanley, open your eyes! You're in a hospital in Tokyo, Japan!" So said the woman in white. I quickly became aware of a pounding headache and tried to feel my head. Numerous bandages startled me on my head that reminded me of my football helmet.

"You received a direct hit on your foxhole by an enemy mortar. It truly is a miracle you've made it this far." I thought about the loaves and fishes. "Carl?" I said. All the nurse could do was shake her head, and tears came to her eyes.

After five days of unconsciousness, being flown by hospital plane from Korea to Japan, all I had was a Purple Heart pinned on my pillow and the thought, "Is Jesus still alive? If so, why isn't Carl?"

Emerson College in Boston

When I returned from Korea in 1954, I was interviewed by a "shaved-head," Second Lieutenant, who, in ninety days, had graduated from Officers Candidate School. He tried to tell me about the benefits of "re-upping" or reenlisting in the Army for another two years. His chest was filled with one ribbon for Good Conduct while my chest had several ribbons, telling a casual viewer that I had seen combat.

After much questioning and trepidation, he realized there was no hope. I would not stay in the Army for any reason. This young boy finally told me that since I was disabled while in the service and not a college graduate, I was eligible to attend any college or university of my choosing and the GI Bill would pay my tuition and books, plus give a stipend of $100 per month for four years or as long as I continuously attended that same institution.

"What school do you want to go to?" the Second Lieutenant asked.

"Can I have a little time to think about it?" After assuring me that he must have his answer in a couple of weeks, I said I would get back to him by phone.

Here I was, a poor Jewish boy from Brooklyn. If someone had made that offer before I went into the Army, was wounded and grown more mature, I would have chosen the Ivy League and Harvard. But since then, I was much older and wiser. This time I chose the Ivy League and Harvard.

What I failed to mention above, is this offer of any college and/or university was contingent upon my being accepted by the school. My high school transcript had more red marks on it than black. My mother was called to school more often than I attended. I was constantly fighting and/or arguing with my

1958 Graduation from Emerson College in Boston
Me, Mom and Pop

fellow students and teachers rather than agreeing with them. I had little chance of being accepted anywhere.

Not being discouraged, I traveled to Boston and to Harvard. The Admissions Officer, after fighting back laughter, told me that I couldn't, nor wouldn't, make it at a prestigious school like Harvard. "Anti-Semite!" I thought (about him and his precious school).

I stayed that night with my cousin Jay, who was attending a small college in the heart of Boston called Emerson College. The school had only three hundred fifty students, mostly girls, since it was just changing into a coed school in order to allow veterans of the Korean War to attend. The next morning I went to see the Admissions Officer of Emerson, was interviewed, toured the school, met several teachers and students and heard about the benefits of a small college. Their acceptance was immediate. I called the Second Lieutenant to let him know.

In September of 1954, I was in a school of twenty-five men and three hundred twenty-five women.

(Boy, this was going to be fun! Maybe I won't get much studying done.) For four years, I was on the Dean's List every year, wore a suit and tie to school every day, graduated with honors, third in my class, was President of the Senior Class and various Veteran groups, learned to play championship bridge, and graduated with a BA degree in Speech and a major in Radio and Television Direction and Production. All this and I couldn't get a job.

Now You Know

"You have an acoustic neuroma, a brain tumor. We won't know if it's cancerous until we take a biopsy when..." my cousin, Dr. Robert Filler's, voice trailed off.

I was looking out the fourth floor window of his office in Boston. There was a cold, almost snowy rain falling in early November. Children and grownups, bundled against the wind, were scurrying to school or work. My thoughts drifted...

I was twenty-six, college educated, had a good job, good family and great prospects. Life was not fair, I thought. I remembered my close buddy in Korea several years before. When I made the same comment to him then, he replied, "If you think life is fair, then you have another thought coming." He was killed in his foxhole the next day.

My random thoughts returned to the problem at hand.

It all makes sense now. The staggering when I danced as if I was drinking but I had had no alcohol. The slight loss of hearing in my right ear. The bleeding from shaving on the right side of my face without even feeling it. The needles in my right arm without any pain. The stubbing of my right big toe, eventually losing the nail, and again with all that numbness.

I don't remember the following several days very well. I returned to New York for a second opinion, told my family, took x-rays, and cleared up my important affairs, not necessarily in that order. I was a zombie going through the motions. I hated the Army for telling me that everything was OK following my battle wound. I hated my mother and father and especially my Aunt Helen for crying. I hated my brother and sister-in-law for trying to be overly cheerful. I hated the people from work for trying to give me a farewell party. Life was definitely not fair.

However, I'm very clear on the next two days even though

they were twenty-one days apart. The day before the operation, my family and some of my friends came to my hospital room. The family sobbed, while my friends made a feeble attempt to remind me of the "good old days" in Brooklyn with my beloved Dodgers. A heavy, black nurse was the only person making sense. Between their noise, she softly told me what was to happen that night and the following dawn. She injected, washed, intravenously fed and answered all my stupid questions. All those final goodbyes were terrible. The clock moved very slowly.

Dinner was liquid. I remember taking fluids in both ends. I lay in this white room counting the holes in the ceiling. And then that smell! In walked Dr. Bronson Ray, my surgeon, with a big, black cigar dangling from the side of his mouth. Although he snuffed it out before entering my room, the smell still lingered in his white coat.

"In my office the other day, you asked me to be frank with you. Not to pull any punches. Well..." he said. I was sorry I said that. "Tomorrow morning about six we will give you a shot to prepare you for the anesthetic. About 7:00AM we will give you ether that will put you to sleep for a good long time. We will open up the back of your head, remove the tumor that has grown around several nerves, quickly have it biopsied, hope that it's not cancerous, make certain we got it all, then close your head up. Now the bad news." You mean it gets worse, I thought.

"Last year, 1958, there were two hundred seventy-six such cases in the world. Only nine are still living." It would have been cocky for me to say, "Well I'm going to be the tenth..." but I couldn't get the words out.

As his last comment penetrated my good half-a-brain, Dr. Ray quickly added, "...but MY batting average was much higher. I performed eleven such operations and five of them still visit my office for regular check-ups. The best of luck to YOU."

I thought, but never said, "And the best of luck to YOU!"

The last visitor to my room was the big, black nurse. She fluffed up my pillow, straightened my sheets, gave me a sleeping pill and leaning over, kissed me on the cheek and said, "Vaya con Dios." How did this woman learn Spanish? She left turning out the lights and closing the door behind her.

I was alone. My family and friends had left. The doctors and nurses had left. My little white room was dark like my heart. There was no hope left as I stared at that little sliver of light from under the door. I cried myself to sleep.

As I said, the next day was twenty-one days later. I was lying on my back. Was this heaven or hell? I was comfortable; I must be in heaven.

I tried to open my eyes to no avail. My right eye was sewed shut; my left was crusted so that any movement of my eyelids was impossible. I felt a soft hand gently caressing mine. I tried to squeeze the strange hand. A commotion ensued. As it turned out it was my Aunt Helen's hand. In astonishment, she had said, "He moved; he moved!" Dr. Ray was summoned.

I smelled that cigar as he grabbed my hand and said, "Stan... Stan..., can you hear me?" I could hear him very clearly but when I tried to talk I became aware of a tube in my throat helping me breathe. I couldn't answer him, though I tried. "Stanley," only when my mother or Aunt Helen was mad at me, did they use that name. Why was Dr. Ray mad at me?

He continued, "...if you can hear me, squeeze my hand!" I followed his instruction. "He did it." Bronson Ray calmly proclaimed. If he smokes another cigar I won't squeeze his hand anymore. "Stan, if your answer to my questions are yes, make a fist and raise your thumb in the air. If no, do nothing. OK?"

I squeezed his hand once more. He let go.

"How do you feel?"

I slowly made a fist and raised my thumb. Everyone was sobbing; maybe even the nurse.

"Are you hungry?"

What a waste of a question, I thought. Of course I was hungry. I vigorously wiggled my thumb. To this day, over forty years later, I still clench my fists and wiggle my thumbs in the air when I'm proud and pleased with myself.

My dad—God love him—said, "I'll get him a corned beef sandwich. He always liked corned beef."

"No, no, Joe! He can't eat that yet," my mother said.

Good old Pop; he was always trying to do good things for me.

"No corned beef for him yet."

Dr. Ray calmly said, "However, there is turkey on today's menu."

In my small, anything but quiet, white hospital room, it was Thursday, November 26, 1959, Thanksgiving Day.

Meeting Pat and Adopting David

After four years of college, two brain operations and various non-directional jobs and girls, I decided to go to California in January of 1963. Of course, there was much wailing from my family and friends but I explained I was in touch with a college friend who assured me I would find a wife in Hollywood. Visiting Aunt Rose, the matriarch of the Cohen family, to say goodbye, she handed me a box that read, "Not to be opened until you get to Jersey and/or beyond." Naturally, I was curious, but complied with my aunt's wishes.

I set out one cold morning, with a small clothes cache, $1000 in cash and my fairly new car, a Chevrolet Corvair convertible in black and red. A good car to win most girls, I thought.

My first stop was a "Jersey" motel where I opened Aunt Rose's box. Amongst fruit and food cans were several rolls of toilet paper. Attached to the paper was a note. "I understand that west of New Jersey, the US is unsettled and filled with Indians. These rolls may be of use. Your loving Aunt, Rose." After that, the rest of the trip was uneventful.

I took a small detour to Las Vegas after four hectic days on the road. I immediately set myself up at a blackjack table where, by 11:00PM, my bankroll had grown to $1500. I called my folks to tell them where I was and of my good fortune. My father advised me to leave Las Vegas immediately. I had never listened to my parents. Why should I start now?

I left Las Vegas the next afternoon, arriving at my friend, Marvin Tabolsky's rented house in the Hollywood Hills. I was broke. Oh, what the hell! I usually was.

Marv had a roommate, George Grippo. After several months of few girls and a job working for the May Co, a branch of a national department store chain, as a carpet salesman, I was restless and lonely. By then my long-time friend, Larry Ross, from Kindergarten in Brooklyn, had joined us and we were then three bachelors on the prowl.

Around Christmas of 1963, Marv and George invited me to a party in some girl's house south of Los Angeles. There were about twenty-five, thirty something people there. After a few hours of boredom, I was approached by this girl, whose only outstanding feature was a gold tooth in the center of her mouth. From all the brainwork on me, I talked out of the side of my mouth, but she looked ridiculous. And she was dressed in a green suit and heels! No one living in casual southern California dressed that way, even on Saturday night.

This is Pat talking now:

I was bored, hadn't met any interesting men, and decided to have one more cup of coffee before leaving. I sat down on a couch next to Stan and, knowing that all men liked to talk about themselves, I asked, "Hi, My name is Pat. What is yours?"

When he answered I thought, Oh, God, he has bad breath! Then, I asked, "And what do you do?"

He answered proudly, "I sell carpets."

Oh Lord, I thought. I can talk about almost any subject in the world, but what can I say about carpets. "Well, what is the most popular color these days?"

"Gold," he replied.

After that, I was at a loss for words and just sat there, fin- ishing my coffee. He finally asked, "Would you like to go for coffee."

Thinking what kind of a dope asks to take a girl for coffee when she has just finished drinking a cup? "Where?"

"Let's go to Scandia's," he replied.

Now, when I was in school at Columbia in New York, people

told me that if I ever had a chance to go with a guy to Scandia's I should say yes. It was an elegant place. So I said, "OK."

Then Stan said, "Your car or my car?"

"I have my own car. Follow me to my place." So Stan followed me to my Westwood Village apartment near UCLA. I parked my car in the assigned underground space and walked to his car.

After I crawled in and he started off to the Hollywood Hills, he said, "Do you like my car?" He was so proud of his blue Chevy convertible.

I said, "Is it paid for?" (Later he said he thought, who on earth has a car that is paid for?)

When Stan said, "No," I said, "Well mine is, I paid cash for my new car."

Later Stan said that he thought, "My God, this girl is really different."

Now go on with his version of the courtship.

Back to Stan's story...

"Hello my name is Pat. And what's yours?" And so started an almost three-year relationship of pleading with her to get married. Pat did so September 1, 1966.

By then, I was working for the Internal Revenue Service (IRS) as a general clerk at $5600 per year. Pat had removed her gold tooth to please me and was teaching at UCLA. We had many discussions on our different religious beliefs, how we would raise the children, etc. I finally had to agree to let her raise the children Catholic. After all, she would be with the kids more than I, since I was working so many hours a week.

After not being accepted by both our families and after not being acceptable to Rabbis and Priests to marry us, we finally were acceptable to a self-declared Justice-of-the Peace in Santa Monica for $25. Larry was my "Best Man" and George was Pat's "Maid of Honor" mainly because our religions coincided. Larry was Jewish and George was a Catholic.

We spent our honeymoon in Acapulco, where it was hot, humid and bug-infested, where Pat made me "schlep" along her typewriter so she could continue writing a chapter of a book on Medical-Surgical Nursing, where the single beds parted and where "skinny-dipping" was observed by teenaged boys. This all contributed to a hilarious (so I thought) beginning of our current forty plus years marriage.

Since we were both thirty-three, we tried having children immediately but we just couldn't "make ends meet." Though physically well, the doctor said we were trying too hard. Really, I was just tired, what with the temperature taking, etc. We decided to adopt. When we were interviewed for our child to be, I told Pat not to worry, that I would "charm" the social worker and she would give us our chosen child. When the day came to pick up David, a three-week old, blonde, blue-eyed Catholic boy, I parked in a "No Parking" zone in front of the Los Angeles Adoption Agency. A motorcycle cop said I would have to move. I answered, "Give me a ticket! I am going to pick up my boy!"

He responded, "I'll watch your car for you."

A Cohen Christmas Story

The phone rang at my desk at the IRS in Los Angeles. It was 2:30PM, December 18, 1969. My neighbor Hal Weber said, "Pat has started labor pains and she has to get to the hospital now! We'll meet you there at four."

I panicked. I had never had the experience of childbirth before since our son, David, was adopted as a baby eighteen months earlier. I told my boss I would be back after the New Year but would check-in daily. I ran for my car.

As usual, traffic was horrific. As I drove toward Kaiser Hospital in Bellflower, my thoughts raced as well. Would the baby (we didn't know the sex) be healthy? Pat had the "Down Syndrome" gene and her sister had just such a boy. The doctors gave us a 50/50 chance.

I arrived at the hospital at four and began the long vigil of hand-squeezing, curses from my wife, name calling, arguments, empty stomachs (mine), full stomachs (Pat's), vomiting, clock-watching and twelve hours of breathless expectations from both of us.

At 5:25AM, December 19th, Susan was born! Being a nurse,

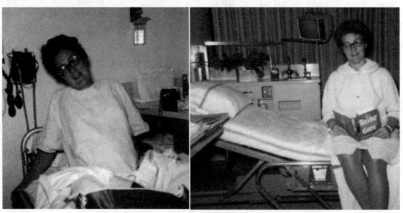

Pat Before Delivery and Pat After Delivery

Pat's first question in the delivery room was, "...does she have ten fingers and ten toes?" With tears clouding my eyes, I counted... "I think so," I said.

At 6:30AM, I went home and collapsed in bed. David was staying with the Webers. I didn't sleep much because of the many phone calls both outgoing and incoming. Pat and Susan came home December 22nd after several days of recuperation from the ordeal. Susan was so tiny that she was dressed in a Santa hat and Christmas stocking.

Then started the merry-go-round of formula-making, diaper-changing, Pat's complaining about uncomfortable stitches, running up and down stairs, David's pneumonia, Susan's crying, meal planning, no cash on hand, phones ringing, and friends trying to help. Our parents were in Brooklyn and Indianapolis.

It was Christmas Eve. Thirty years ago there were no ATM's and we didn't have any credit cards. Banks closed on holidays and I forgot to cash my paycheck. What a holiday! How could anyone be jolly?

I broke open David's piggy bank and took the 512 pennies. I found a Chinese restaurant open on Christmas Eve and luckily they took my pennies. We ate our cold chow mein and wished each other a merry Christmas.

About midnight, David, in the crib next to Pat, stopped his coughing, Susan fell asleep in my wife's arms and Pat could no longer stay awake. I looked at my little family all snuggled in their warm beds. Tears came to my eyes from exhaustion and happiness. There were no trees, no lights or wreaths, neither mistletoe nor stockings, just quiet Christmas music coming from our radio.

It was truly a Silent night... a Holy night.

They'll Never Convict Me!

CHAPTER THIRTEEN

As stated in various television dramas, "The following story contains scenes of frontal nudity; parental discretion is advised."

Several months before, Pat and I had our second child, Susan, a bouncing happy girl giving us the perfect family—a boy, David, of two years and now a girl of six months. David was adopted as a week-old, blonde boy, from the Los Angeles Adoption Agency and then as usually happens, Pat became pregnant and our family was completed.

We decided that we would not risk having any more children so Pat and I discussed having either her "tubes tied" or a vasectomy for me. As usual, I won (or lost)! It was me that would be medically "fixed." After all, remember, she was the Catholic and did not want to feel guilty. I was the Jew in the partnership. That's why I lost (or won)!

We both visited our HMO, Kaiser, and our favorite doctor, who interviewed us, had both of us sign the necessary papers, and made the appointment to have the vasectomy done. We selected a Friday in April where I would recuperate over the weekend and return to work on Monday. I was employed at the Internal Revenue Service and since April was "filing month" I should only be on leave for one day.

The morning of the procedure, I awoke at 4:00AM after not sleeping much. The usual thoughts kept me awake. Would it hurt? When can I urinate again? Would my recuperation be as predicted? Would I hurt? What if the procedure didn't "take" and Pat became pregnant again? Would I hurt?

I quickly showered and shaved (must look good for all the nurses that would be watching) all while Pat slept. Sure, why should she worry! I was the one to be scarred for life. The children were thankfully quiet.

I left the house at five for the forty-five minute ride to Kaiser Bellflower where the operation was to be performed. I neither ate nor drank anything per the doctor's orders. Didn't want me throwing up all over my soon-to-be-taken maleness. Oh, what a mistake I made agreeing to this.

Arriving just before six, I checked in and was led to an anti-room next to the surgery amphitheater. I then was told those famous words by a pretty, young nurse, "Take ALL your clothes off and put on this gown with the ties in the back!" This nurse said the words matter-of-factly as if she has said them thousands of times. Sure, I thought. Means nothing to her. Bet she sees naked men everyday. I wonder if she says those words to her boyfriend.

Satan himself must have designed these gowns. I had trouble knotting the ties in the back. I tied one or two. The heck with it. It was my front I wanted to protect.

Into my room walked a man pushing a Gurney in front of him. Was he also going to see me naked, I thought? Maybe he was gay. He asked me to lie on the Gurney, face up, so I didn't have to worry about my exposed rear. The man rolled me next door to Surgery and left. As if I wasn't nervous enough, under those powerful lights that shown directly in my eyes, I nearly panicked. I thought of jumping up and calling this whole foolish thing off. Before I completed my thoughts, into the room walked about a hundred people, or what appeared to be far too many onlookers.

There was the surgeon, young (about twelve, I thought), his nurse, the good-looking young blonde that told me to take all my clothes off, and many, many others who all wanted a look at my private parts. All were wearing their Lone Ranger masks that made them look like Halloween characters. "Stan," the surgeon said, "I'm Dr. Jeff (something) and this is my head nurse, Cathy O'Brien." Oh fine, I thought, a good Catholic who hates Jews. "These other men and women are learning the intricacies of this procedure and I asked them to join me. Do you mind?"

What was I to say, yes I mind? I don't want them to look at the little thing I have? "No," I blurted out. "Let's get on with it."

Was it ever cold in that room, especially when the surgeon removed my gown. I lay there completely exposed for those hundred people to see, plus the rest of the world. Pat should be here to hold my hand. One more female wouldn't make any difference. Next time, I'll insist Pat have the operation. At least I would hold her hand.

I had my knees up with my feet on the table. The pretty blonde, Lone Ranger nurse separated my knees and began swabbing between my legs with iodine. The hundred sightseers bent closer to get a better look. There goes the little bit of modesty I had left. The surgeon then said, "Stan, I'm going to give you some local anesthetic to numb the area. It will take a few seconds for it to take effect. When it does, believe me you won't feel a thing!" I felt a little sharp sting as I was stuck with a needle. I wonder where he put the needle.

While waiting for the anesthetic to take effect, he made some small talk to distract me from the hundred onlookers. "What kind of work do you do?" he asked. I thought for a moment then didn't answer. Louder he repeated, "What do you do for a living?"

Another moment passed and I mumbled, "You don't want to know!"

"What did you say, Stan?" the surgeon asked.

I answered louder this time, "You don't want to know and I'd rather not tell you!"

"Oh come on Stan, it can't be that bad."

It's much worse than that, I thought. I mumbled, "I work for the IRS."

"What was that Stan?" reaching for his instruments.

I nearly shouted, "I'm an Agent for the Internal Revenue Service."

A hush fell over the gathered multitude.

"Would you mind repeating that again?" he said, reaching for his scalpel.

"I'm a collection agent for the IRS!" I yelled.

The surgeon paused as he in turn looked at the knife in his hand and my bare "jewels" in front of him. At first he murmured, "They'll never convict me! They'll never convict me!" Then louder he said, "My peers in the jury will understand this in April, I had a scalpel and my patient collected taxes for the IRS. They'll understand."

I fainted.

I awoke seconds later to hear humming from the surgeon, mixed laughter and murmurs from the "street people" and the blonde nurse saying to the surgeon, "You have to tell your fellow doctors in the Cafeteria about this. They wouldn't believe it." I collapsed again!

I finally awoke again in the anti-room where the big black man was standing over me with a big smile on his face. "How do you feel, Mr. Cohen?" He paused, waiting for an answer. When none was forthcoming he continued. "You're the talk of the Hospital already. You and Dr. Jeff (something). Is it true? Are you with the IRS?" Very funny, I thought. I reached down between my legs to see if I had anything left. "No, no! You can't touch yourself there yet. Your hands may not be sterile." My hands may not be sterile, but my you-know-what is, I thought, if there's anything left.

"You take a little nap for a while and then the surgeon wants to talk to you. Then you can go home," he said. I bet he's having a good laugh down in the Cafeteria, I thought.

After hurting, staring at the ceiling, feeling sticky in that area, but mostly hurting, in walked the surgeon with a big smile on his face. "Now," he said, "lets' see how we're doing."

What is this *we* business. Don't *we* me. "I'm doing terrible," I mumbled.

"Nice, nice..." he said, looking at his butchery. "Everything looks fine."

Proud of yourself, eh. Well, I hurt and am embarrassed. But, the worst was yet to come.

"Take some of these pads," he said, reaching into the supply closet, "and change them about four times per day, when they become bloody." I fainted again—or nearly so. They were women's sanitary pads or Kotex!

"Do I have to wear those," I said, "are they necessary?"

"Can't be beat for keeping your underwear dry. Leave it to women. They always know what's good for us men!"

"Now, you can head home, but take it very easy. You're going to feel 'blah' for a few days, but you should be back to normal in a few short days. You can have sex when you feel up to it. Eat normally but drink loads of fluids. You can go back to work anytime starting next week. Are there any questions?"

"Yes," I said, "How do you people sleep at night?"

Sts. Simon & Jude Church

We moved to Huntington Beach with David in September 1969. Pat joined Sts. Simon and Jude Church, a Franciscan Catholic Church, where she said the priests were more liberal than the Los Angeles Diocese.

Since she was not married in the Church, Pat was denied the sacraments, which included the receiving of Communion. She continued to "practice" her faith each week without being fulfilled.

In 1971, we met Father Ronald Colloty, the Pastor, who agreed to marry us. The only question he had of me was how I was going to raise David and Susan. So, in 1971, five years after our original "handholding" and with David as my new "Best Man" and Susan, Pat's new "Maid of Honor," we were officially married in the Catholic Church. I loved Pat, as much, if not more, than the first time we were married.

And so it began. Pat and I became involved in numerous activities with the parish.

Along with Pat, we were asked by Sister Maureen, the head nun of Sts. Simon and Jude Church to carry the "offerings" to the alter. I reminded her that I was not a Catholic and she said, "So what!" I went with Pat to Mass every Saturday night and was soon told by the priests that I attended church more often than the majority of their parishioners. Pat and I also occasionally attended the Jewish Friday night services at a local synagogue to keep our lives as balanced as possible. Pat liked the Jewish prayers and wanted me to know the rabbi and some of the congregation members.

On Christmas of one year, I was asked to carry a flag into Church to tell the people that Christ was born. Pat and I were asked to teach those of the Catholic faith how two people,

1971, David 18 mos., Pat and Susan 3 mos.

of different faiths, could remain together in marriage. It was a series of "B" Team group meetings. The "B" Team stood for "Betrothal Team" and there would be about sixty to seventy young couples attending Sts. Simon and Jude Church meeting hall. I kept kidding the leader that I wanted to make the "A" Team. How could I do that?

Also, I was asked to collect the over $100,000 in moneys collected at the "Fall Festivals" held by the Church Volunteers. My friend, John Warco, said that they trusted a Jew more than some of their own parishioners to do it.

After Pat's mother died, I went to weekly Mass with Pat to help her get over her grief remembering her mother being at her side during the Mass. Pat was grateful, but she later regretted making the mistake of taking me along to a Mass on Holy Thursday. At that time, Sister Maureen was in charge of arranging the liturgy and she had decided to have parishioners play the parts of Christ, Herod and the Jewish rabble. I became angry when I heard the actors repeat, "Crucify Him, Crucify Him" and I left the Mass and waited for Pat in the car. I never went back to church with her for many years. One day I finally told Maureen why I wasn't coming with Pat to church anymore, and she said at that time in Jerusalem, the people were Jews and that was the truth. I told her that even if it were true, this is the 20th Century and she didn't have to say it aloud to foster more anti-Semitism than already existed in this Country. In recent years, the Pope changed the Gospel and the celebration of Holy Thursday to say it was the people of the time who crucified Jesus.

1991, Stan and Pat remarried at their 25th Wedding Anniversary

And finally, in 1991, twenty-five years after our original wedding ceremony before the Justice-of-the Peace in Santa Monica, we were "remarried" in the Church by the same priest who married us at Sts. Simon and Jude Church in 1971, Father Ron Colloty.

My fondest wish is that God loves Pat as much as I do.

In 1994 I began working for the Orange County Register's newly formed local for Huntington Beach, called *The Wave*. It was suggested by one of my readers that I write a story for the National Legacy writing contest. The Board of that Leibowitz Foundation believed that if Jewish old folks would write stories from their lives during the holocaust, the act of writing would help them heal. My wonderful wife, Pat, who didn't believe I had any writing talent at all, pooh-poohed the idea, so without telling her, I wrote a three-page story and entered it into the local contest. It won for me $150! Well, that surprised both of us. Then without telling me, the local judges entered my story in the National Legacy contest. Some months later I received a letter announcing that I had won first prize and $5000! The Judges said that they had never read a story that caused them to both laugh and cry in the same three-page story. Of course my loving wife Pat immediately confiscated the check and put the money in her savings account! Here is that winning story.

Confessions of a Tax Collector
or the Tale of the Erroneous Refund

When I began working for the IRS in the 60s, one of my first assignments as a Collections Officer was to attempt to collect "Erroneous Refunds." Sometimes a taxpayer filed his personal tax return and asked for a refund of monies that he may have overpaid during the year. Occasionally, the IRS would send back to the taxpayer the wrong amount. It was my assignment to collect these erroneous amounts sent to taxpayers ONLY when the amount returned to the taxpayer was MORE than the amount that was due. The IRS couldn't be bothered with underpayments.

One day I received a "bill" (amount erroneously refunded) on a single gentleman named Hector Fernandez, I think. At least it was a Spanish surname. He lived at 814½ Crescent Lane in Santa Ana. What caught my eye was the "one-half." In those days, anyone who lived behind a house with a "whole" number was usually poor. Anyway, Mr. Fernandez had asked for a refund of $200 and had received a check for $25,200 approximately 18 months before. The IRS would let Mr. Fernandez keep any interest that he had gained from the extra monies, since it was our mistake, but we just wanted the over-payment of the $25,000.

That morning, I went to the given address, and just as I figured, it was a "run-down shack" behind a fairly decent home. The front door appeared to be off its hinges and might fall when I even knocked on the door. I tapped, hesitantly. After a few moments, the door opened slightly and without seeing the person inside, I asked, "Mr. Fernandez?" Noisily, the door opened outwardly.

Hector Fernandez was a thin man, about 75 years old, needed a shave and was in a wheelchair. Looking down at him, I said, "I'm Stan Cohen from the Internal Revenue Service. Can I come in?" Nervously, I fumbled with my credentials and business card, placing both in his lap. "Yes, please do, come in," he said, returning my identification and wheeling smartly around to let me follow him inside. "I've been expecting you." The door closed behind me.

I was in a one-room house with an oil cloth—ask your grandma what oil cloth is—covering a kitchen table. It had numerous pictures of an older woman and a younger family, which took up most of the space on the table. In this one room, there was a small, dirty stove and sink, and an old Army cot, apparently where Mr. Fernandez slept. I saw no toilet. Next to the cot, I saw a small suitcase, which appeared to be full.

"Before you do what you have to do," he said in a heavily accented voice, "I would like to tell you a little story. Would you join me in a cup a tea."

"If you have coffee, instant would be fine," I answered. What a dumb thing for me to ask, I thought.

He quickly prepared the drinks for us and began his story. I listened without interrupting.

"About a year and a half ago, I sent in my Income Tax Return, asking for a refund of $200. My wife of 42 years died 12 years ago and left me some ATT stock. That's a picture of her." He pointed to the picture of the older woman on our table.

"ATT withholds some of my dividends for tax payments and that year, they sent you people too much. I asked for $200 back."

I sipped my lukewarm, instant coffee that was much too strong. Mr. Fernandez continued.

"After a few months, I received this check in the mail from the IRS. I didn't look at the amount, thinking it was my refund for $200. I took it to my bank on the corner, filled out the deposit slip for $200 and went to the teller. When she looked at the check and the deposit slip, she told me the check was for $25,200, not just $200. Somebody had made a terrible mistake. I only thought I was getting $200 back, and now I had all this money. I wheeled over to my friend, the bank manager."

I couldn't handle much more coffee. I put down the cup.

"The bank manager told me he had heard about the IRS sending too much money, and if I wanted to deposit this check in the bank, I could keep any money it made in interest, and then just pay back the original amount they sent me by mistake. Was he right?"

I broke my silence. "He was absolutely correct. All we wanted…" He interrupted me. He had gotten new confidence.

"I didn't think that I should take all that money. I took the check home and mailed it back to the return address on the envelope. About a month later, the same check for $25,200 came back with no explanation. I called the phone number listed in the newspaper and spoke to the woman. She said to put a note with the check with my name, address and Social Security number in another envelope and mail it to her and she would take care of it. I did that, and in another month, a new check came in the mail for $25,200, the same amount."

I fidgeted in my chair; the coffee made me need to go to the bathroom.

"I called my daughter, that's her family there, she said I should deposit the money in the bank and wait until I received another letter. I did that and you are the first one I have heard from the IRS since then."

"Fine," I said. "All you need do now, is write me a check for $25,000 and I'll be on my way."

"But there's more to the story," he said.

"Oh, oh, here it comes," I said under my breath. I was quiet again.

"After I deposited the money in the bank, the monthly bank

statements began coming in; first, $25,950, then $27,005 and so on. Here was all this money sitting there, not doing nothing. I thought much about that money. I called my daughter, who agreed with me."

"I am 77 years old, in a wheelchair, not feeling well; I could not spend too much time in jail before I died. I decided to spend the money!" He said it as if he were very proud of himself; he went on.

"All my life I wanted to see the world, see those places I've just read about. Travel the world. That's what I did with your money. I got a ticket, first class, to go around the world on the Queen Elizabeth II for 65 days. I went to Hawaii, Tahiti, Fiji, Tokyo, Bangkok, Indonesia, Calcutta, Israel, Egypt, France, England, New York, Florida, through the Panama Canal and then back here to Los Angeles." He spoke much quicker and louder.

"They all treated me like a King. I went first class, you remember. A steward was assigned to me, just to take me and show me all these places. I saw that lady's palace in India, the Pope on the balcony in Rome (Mr. Fernandez made the sign of the cross), those guards at the Queen's Home in London. It was like a fairy tale come true." He stopped. There was a far-away look in his eyes.

He paused. His voice was lower again. The heavy accent returned. He wheeled over to the packed suitcase, put it on his lap, wheeled back to the table, and opened the suitcase. It was full with all the paraphernalia needed for a 'round-the-world' trip. Besides the colorful brochures and pictures, there were a few clothes and some toilet articles in the suitcase. "Here are all the pamphlets, brochures and receipts for the money I spent." Mr. Fernandez paused, looking at the brochures longingly.

"Here is the last statement I received last week from the bank. It shows only $7,892.14 left. I'm ready, Mr. Cohen. Take me to jail." Mr. Fernandez, head down, put his two wrists together and wept.

It was difficult looking at him through MY glazed eyes. I thought for what seemed a very long time. I still had to go to the toilet.

After a few minutes, I said, "Mr. Fernandez, give me back my business card."

He fumbled with the papers in front of him. "I don't understand," he said.

"Give me back my card, " I repeated. "If anyone should ask, you never saw me or heard from the IRS. Do you understand?"

"Yes," he replied, "but what are you going to do?"

I rose, "Thank you for the coffee," I said and left his room. Those were the last words I ever spoke to or heard from Mr. Fernandez.

After a trip to the bathroom, I returned to my office and wrote my report: "Hector Fernandez, 814½ Crescent Avenue, Santa Ana, CA 92701, SSN 567-22-1034. Unable to Locate."

CHAPTER SIXTEEN

Confessions of a Tax Collector
or the Ginsburg Bakery Story

It was lunchtime on a lazy Friday in early October at the IRS. My partner, Eli, and I were looking forward to celebrating the Jewish New Year (Rosh Hashanah) that night with our families.

We were working the big "Trust Fund" cases that needed immediate attention. If a business failed to turn over to the Internal Revenue Service their "trust fund" monies, money that the company took from their employees for withholding taxes, in a timely fashion, Eli and I would visit the business and collect a cashiers check for the back trust funds or close the business until the delinquent amount was paid. We had settled most of our cases for that week.

As we were about to leave for lunch with a few general cases to wind down the week, the boss called us into his office. He threw a new case at us and said, "Don't come back to this office without a cashiers check or the keys." He always said that. A nicer boss didn't exist.

The case was on "Ginsburg's Bakery" on Harbor Blvd. in Costa Mesa for $62,012 for three quarters (¾ of a year) of unpaid trust fund taxes. "Hey boss," Eli said, "I shop there! This is a Jewish bakery. This is the day before the Jewish New Year,

> By 1970, I had been working as an Internal Revenue Officer in Los Angeles. My partner was Eli Ornstein, a retired Naval officer who was filling in his later years by working at the IRS as well. We became good friends and partners. This story is about one of our cases.

a bakery's busiest day of the year. We'll see them Monday."

The boss replied "You'll collect it today. We show no favorites here at the IRS. And what better team to work the case but two Jew boys."

Maybe he wasn't that great after all. We protested to no avail. Eli and I left the office mumbling.

It was 11:45AM. We went to our Government car and immediately to Costa Mesa and the bakery. Nothing was going to prevent us from getting home on time that night.

As we expected, Ginsburg's Bakery was jammed. There were at least six women working behind a small glass case that exhibited the bakery's great cakes and breads. There were at least three times that amount of men and women shoppers trying to buy Ginsburg's products, by raising their hands and shouting. "I'm next!" was mingled with the sound of the cash registers. And then there was that smell! A smell of a Jewish bakery with fresh breads and cakes is like none other. Once you smell that smell, you never forget it.

"Where's the boss?" I shouted to one of the women behind the case. She pointed to a staircase leading upstairs to a closed door. The stairs were flour covered and slippery and Eli and I carefully opened the door.

In a small room, at a desk covered with papers and flour, sat Mr. Ginsburg. The smallish man with a big nose didn't even look up when he said, "I'm busy! Come back later!" Eli stuck his IRS badge under that big nose and the smallish old man slowly looked up. "Yes, yes fellas, for you I'll make time. A schtickle of challah?" He was munching on Jewish bread.

"No thanks," Eli said as we sat down on two floured chairs. "Mr. Ginsburg, you are Mr. Ginsburg, I presume?" Ginsburg nodded. Eli continued. "I'm Eli Ornstein and this is Stan Cohen and we are from the IRS. There is the matter of your taxes, your trust fund taxes of $62,012 from last October to last June. Have they been paid?"

Coolish days didn't matter. Mr. Ginsburg began to sweat. "Not exactly," Ginsburg said.

"What do you mean, not exactly?" I said.

Ginsburg replied, "I was just working on them today and will send in a check next week, after the holidays. You two nice Jewish boys understand that I make the most money of the year during Rosh Hashanah and Yom Kippur—just like Christmas you know." He wiped his forehead. "You sure you don't want a piece of bread or any other cake downstairs?"

I remembered that smell as it came up though the spaces in the slats of the floor. It was lunchtime and hard saying no.

I rose and brushed the flour spots off my suit. Walking to the window of the small office, I said, "Mr. Ginsburg, please come here." Ginsburg came to the window. "Do you see that Locksmith truck in you parking lot?"

"Yes." Ginsburg said.

"Well, the locksmith in that truck is watching this window. If I give him a signal, he will come into your bakery, shoo all the customers and employees out, change all the locks on the doors, and place this sign on your front door." From his briefcase, Eli produced a cardboard, one foot square sign with large red lettering that read

THIS LOCATION IS NOW US GOVERNMENT PROPERTY! IT HAS BEEN SEIZED FOR FAILURE TO PAY FEDERAL TAXES! ANY TRESPASSING BY UNAUTHORIZED PERSONS IS PUNISHABLE BY FEDERAL LAWS!

Mr. Ginsburg gulped and sweated more. "You nice Jewish boys wouldn't do that! Not before the Jewish holidays. Here, here..." he rushed to his desk, "...here, I will write you a check today for the full amount!!!" He began writing.

Eli said, "Mr. Ginsburg. It's lunchtime and Mr. Cohen and I are going to have a sandwich next door. We will be back at 1:15. At that time, you will give us a cashiers check for $62,012, to repeat a *cashiers check* or cash for $62,012 by 1:15 or we will have to ask the locksmith to join us. Do you understand?"

"Yes, yes," Ginsburg said, "but you know I can't raise that kind of money in just an hour!"

I said, "1:15," and started walking down the stairs. The door slammed behind us. Oh those smells.

Eli and I ate our sandwiches rather quietly, discussing plans for that night. We returned to Ginsburg's office and met Mr. Asher, Ginsburg's attorney. Mr. Asher pleaded with Eli and me to give the bakery more time to come up with the $62,000. We sat stoically. Mr. Asher, seeing that his pleas were falling on deaf ears, produced his personal check for $62,012. "You can bet that this check has enough money behind it so you needn't worry about the check bouncing. Mr. Ginsburg and I just haven't had sufficient time to get your cashiers check." Eli and I spoke quietly to each other.

I continued. "We will accept this check now. On Monday, I will go to the bank and attempt to have this personal check converted to a cashiers check. If I can, you will hear no more from the IRS until next month. If I am unable to convert it, Mr. Ornstein and I will return Monday morning with the Locksmith to close your doors. Is that fully understood?"

"Yes, yes," Mr. Ginsburg said, "You can be sure, it'll be good, it'll be good. Thank you both very much." As we walked down the stairs, Mr. Ginsburg yelled, "Happy holidays to you both!"

As I drove Eli to his car at the Federal Building, we discussed the case. "I will call the boss and tell him we collected the money from the bakery but that we got hung up and didn't have time to return to the office. Monday, I will take the personal check, hopefully have it converted to a cashier's check and then bring it to the boss and tell him we got it on Friday. OK?" Eli agreed. I wished him a good holiday season and went home.

Monday morning, everything fell into place. I saw the boss about 10:30AM and showed him the cashier's check. "Just another notch in our gun," I flippantly said as I left his office.

That afternoon the boss called Eli and me into his office. Smilingly, he said, "In looking at the cashier's check for $62,012 from Ginsburg's Bakery, I noticed that it had today's date on it. How come?"

He was a nice boss.

The J. Paul Getty Story

In the early 1970s, after about five years working for the IRS, I was promoted to a "Senior Revenue Officer" and was assigned to work the downtown Los Angeles area. I was given Taxpayer Delinquent Accounts (TDAs), or collection bills, on some of the very large legal or accounting firms downtown. Occasionally, I would receive a TDA on a famous actor or corporation president who had used his accounting firm's address as his own.

On this day, I received a bill for J. Paul Getty, the famous billionaire, who used the address of his Arthur Anderson Accounting firm located downtown. Several notices plus a Certified Letter had been sent to this accounting firm with apparently no response. That morning I visited Arthur Anderson, Inc., one of the "Big Seven" for the first time.

I entered the very large, ornate lobby of the firm. There was just one person sitting behind a round desk in the center of a spacious room. Giant pictures, overstuffed chairs, couches and tables surrounded this desk. The lobby was filled with mostly well-dressed men and one or two women smoking, chatting and pacing (some of them). The desk occupant wore a telephone headset and she was constantly talking into it. I approached her and when she paused, I bent over the desk and whispered, "My name is Stan Cohen, and I would like to see someone who handles the J. Paul Getty account."

"What?" she answered. "Speak a little louder." She was interrupted by another ringing telephone.

Again I said, this time a little louder, "I am from the IRS. Could you…"

"Please, speak up!" So at the top of my voice, I shouted, "J. Paul Getty owes $42 million dollars to the IRS! Would you please write me a check!"

The lobby became silent; the people stopped talking and pacing; the phones stopped ringing. "Could you please repeat that sir?" she said with astonishment. And then in the midst of the silence, she said, "Yes, sir, I'll have someone here in a moment," she answered.

In what seemed like no more than ten seconds, a young man with his hair and tie both askew, met me at the center desk. "Yes, I handle Mr. Getty's taxes; what can I do for you?" he said nonchalantly, looking more at his papers than at me.

With growing annoyance, I said, "I am from the IRS. Mr. Getty owes $42 million on his personal income tax for 1969 and I'm here to collect." I showed him my credentials and impatience at the same time.

Excitedly, he said, "Step right this way sir. I'll have you speak to our Vice-President, Mr. Orville Carpenter, who is in charge of Mr. Getty's tax returns." We left the lobby and I was led through two gigantic oak doors. "Right in there." the young man said. I entered a large office with a secretary sitting between me and two more large doors. The big oak doors closed behind me and the gentleman had disappeared.

"Yes sir, can I help you?" Hilda Franks, the secretary inquired without looking up from her typing.

"I'd like to see Mr. Carpenter." I said.

She, very efficiently, asked, "and what is this concerning?" Again my credentials and my impatience were both shown.

"Look, lady. I'm from the Collection Division of the Internal Revenue Service. Mr. J. Paul Getty owes $42 million in back taxes and I was told that Mr. Carpenter could write me a check for that amount. I will walk out of here this morning with either a cashier's check for that amount or the keys for this building!"

"Just a minute, sir," she said, hesitantly. She stopped typing immediately and called her boss. "You can go right in, sir."

I remember thinking she must have been afraid to rise from her chair.

Another big office, more pictures and more over-stuffed furniture confronted me. But this time, a middle-aged well-dressed man (with a vest) said, "Hello. I'm Orv Carpenter. What seems to be the problem? Won't you have a seat." Now, this was what an executive should look like and talk like, I thought. Mr. Carpenter stood behind his desk, framed by a picture window.

I explained the reason for my visit; it seemed like the twentieth time. Orv, as he asked me to call him, chuckled. "Happens all the time," he said, asking me to bring my chair and sit with him behind his desk. "Watch this." he said.

Loudly, he shouted into the phone. "Hilda, I want to see the entire staff on the J. Paul Getty account with a copy of Mr. Getty's 1969 Income Tax Return in my office in sixty seconds. Do you understand?" He slammed down the phone. We heard scurrying about behind the oak doors. Smiling and in a more pleasant tone, he said to me, "Watch what happens now. We are going to have some fun!"

In what seemed about ten seconds, the big oak doors swung open and, led by Ms. Franks, seven senior men and younger men in various types of business suits, literally ran into the room. When the commotion subsided, Hilda spoke. "Mr. Carpenter, here is the entire staff. Is there anything else?" She didn't wait for an answer but turned and scurried from the room. The seven men standing attention like soldiers were flanked by a gray haired man in a vested suit at one end and by a very young man with disheveled hair and suit at the other.

After a pause, Mr. Carpenter spoke slowly, calmly and clearly. "This gentleman sitting beside me is from the Internal Revenue Service. He says there is a mathematical mistake in Mr. Getty's 1969 return. The amount owed to the IRS by this firm and Mr. Getty is $42 million. Mr. Cohen also says that many notices have been sent to this firm asking for an explanation of this deficit and the IRS has never received a single reply." His voice was rising. "Now what in the world is going on here? If all of you want to continue our long term relationship at this firm, you'd better come up with an immediate explanation."

Silence. The large room fell silent. Again ten seconds passed. The "vest" was the first to speak. Turning to his left, and raising his voice to the man standing next to him, he said, "That man sitting with Mr. Carpenter is from the IRS. He says that Mr. Getty owes $42 million dollars. What in the world is going on here?"

The second man spoke to the third man in the same tone, asking for the same explanation. And so on, down the line again, like soldiers. Each passed along the same question until it reached the disheveled young man at the end of the line. Since he had no one to pass along the question, after a pause, he spoke. "I will find out the reason for this discrepancy, if I may return in a few minutes?"

"Go, all of you, and be back in thirty minutes with an explanation or your resignation papers!" Orv said loudly to them all. "Thirty minutes!" The line broke up and the staff, led by the "vest" left through the big oak doors. The room was quiet again. "Let's get a cup of coffee in the Executive Lunch Room. Trust me. We will have your answer in thirty minutes or sooner."

After small talk over coffee upstairs, we returned to Mr. Carpenter's office to meet the sloppily dressed young man and Ms. Franks. "Mr. Franks has all the documents and the complete explanation of the problem." Hilda Franks left the room and the young man, smiling, began his explanation.

The next morning I strolled into my IRS and was immediately confronted by my supervisor. "How did you make out on the Getty problem, yesterday?"

"Bad news, Boss," I said smiling. "I'll be in your office in a second with the full explanation." After putting down my briefcase and gathering all the papers on the Getty case, I went to my supervisor's office. He had made coffee, so I helped myself to a cup. "The bottom line is they wrote the $42 million on the wrong line. They mistakenly wrote $42 million was owed when it should have been $42 million was to be refunded. It seems we owe HIM $42 million dollars instead of him owing us that amount."

"Great… just great!" my boss remarked, sarcastically.

Golf

David and Susan were jumping on the beds of this small motel near San Diego. It was 8:30AM on a beautiful Easter vacation day in 1975, and Pat and I had promised the children to take them to Sea World during their days off from school.

The four of us had driven down from our Huntington Beach home (about a hundred miles) the previous night and the neighbor couple and their two children had met us at the motel. I wasn't anxious to go to Sea World, what with all the fish and children, so I asked Pat if she would go with the other couple while I played golf in the area. She replied, "O.K., if you must. But you better be back by 4:00PM." I promised I would.

I journeyed to the nearby and famous Torrey Pines Golf Club for a day of golf. It was a beautiful day and an equally beautiful course. It wasn't very crowded but the Green Fees were a little steep, $15.00, for a weekday on a public course. When I approached the "starter," there were a few men milling around the pro shop but no one at the counter. I said I was a "single" and I would play alone or with anyone.

The starter said, "Do you mind playing with that threesome now on the first tee?" He pointed to the three men poised to tee off.

"No! Not at all." I proceeded to the first tee.

As I approached the men, I noticed they all looked familiar but I hesitated in identifying them. Suddenly, I realized who one gentleman was, Peter Falk from the movies and television. Immediately, I wanted to ask Mr. Falk for his autograph but since I was to play a round of golf with him and his buddies that may last at least four hours, I didn't ask then. I then realized who the other two men were John Cassevettes and John Williams, both famous actors and orchestra leaders in their own rights. I was excited and thrilled but I was determined not to show my awe.

I introduced myself as "Stan" to them and they in turn mentioned their first names only. We all teed off. I was first. I had a "handicap" of around fifteen, or my rounds averaged somewhere in the nineties, depending on the course and if I had an argument with my wife the night before. I drove my first shot with a little slice about 175 yards on the 425 yard, par four, first hole. Peter and the two John's all went about the same distance and in the wide fairway.

We plodded on, taking turns on scores of 4s thru 7s on each of the next four holes. It was fairly slow play but not as slow as the courses in Orange and Los Angeles Counties. On the fifth hole, a short 195-yard hole, over the Pacific Ocean, we waited on a bench for the foursome in front of us to clear the green.

Peter Falk said to me, "I can't stand it anymore! Don't you know who I am or my friends?"

I responded, "Yes, you all look a little familiar but I hesitated on saying something for fear I was wrong." I knew exactly who they all were.

"I'm Peter Falk from TV and that's John Cassevettes and John Williams also on TV!"

"That's nice," I said, "do you recognize me?"

"No, should I?" Peter said.

"I'm Stan Cohen from the IRS!" I said.

From there on there was a "running" joke between myself and the other three on their notoriety and my official position with the Internal Revenue Service. We kidded back and forth on their failure to pay taxes and/or their apparent failure to pay the correct amounts. I kept threatening to call the police to arrest the bad taxpayers and saying that if I didn't turn them all in, I would not continue to work for the IRS. I had shown them my "credentials" and pretended to take their fingerprints.

Peter Falk kept introducing me to other people on the

course as "…that detective from the IRS." John Williams told me of a concert he starred in but wasn't paid and asked if I could do anything about it. And so on throughout the entire round of golf.

On one hole, after I had hit a 165-yard, 5-iron shot onto the green, John Cassevettes asked if he could borrow my club. While swinging, he was distracted by the bindings on my club beginning to unravel. He said, "Don't we pay you enough to buy some new, half decent clubs?"

I said in response, "I only make about $25,000 a year at the IRS."

John Williams piped up and said, "I make that in one night." I talked into my watch as if I was giving someone else that information.

On another hole, Peter Falk had driven into a bunch of big lawn mowers with elongated wings that quickly cut his ball in two. When he saw this, he turned to me and asked, "Is this deductible?"

At around 2:00PM, we finished the 18th hole. We had all shot in the 90s, some low some high. I thought the scores should have been higher but Peter was scoring.

John Williams said, "Please join us for a beer in the clubhouse."

Remembering Pat's warning and glancing at my watch, I agreed.

When I told them that I didn't drink and ordered an ice tea Peter Falk said to the surrounding golfers, "Would you believe an IRS man who doesn't drink?"

I was embarrassed, but the other three had to sign autographs. No one asked me for mine.

About 3:00PM, I had to excuse myself to get back to the motel and to Pat and the kids. We shook hands all around and said our farewells.

A more glorious day of golf I had never had nor was I ever to have, except when I shot a legitimate 81 on the Wilson Course in Los Angeles. All three men were gracious and most ordinary in spite of their prominence in public. It was truly a pleasure and a privilege to spend six hours with them even though I never asked them for their autographs.

A Pilgrim's Tour of the Holy Land

In March 2005, I finally agreed to take a trip to Israel and Jerusalem. I have always hesitated because of the dangerous situation in Israel and the fact that it was "sponsored" by the Catholic Church. I was afraid someone would try to convert me. But my wife convinced me that I should go because she had always wanted to and now that she had cancer, she might not ever have the chance again. So we set off on this nineteen member pilgrimage with Father Christian and seventeen other Catholics. I was the only Jew.

A non-stop flight to Newark, New Jersey, several delays, and then another non-stop flight to Tel Aviv. A nice hotel and a kosher breakfast followed. We had Catholic morning prayers on the bus and set off on our tour. The second and third nights were spent at a Jewish Kibbutz near the Sea of Galilee. A strange place for a Catholic group, I thought.

I was baptized for the second time (You remember the first time was in my *Water, Water, Everywhere* story). This time in the Jordan River where Jesus was baptized, Father Christian Mondor, Priest from Sts. Simon and Jude Church in Huntington Beach, threw "holy" water on me with an olive branch because, as he said later, "You were the only one in the group who was unwashed!"

Every day we had Mass, and Father Chris said a special prayer for me while holding my head in his hands. Every day I was extremely moved, occasionally to tears.

We visited the Masada, a mountain fortress where Herod tried to eliminate the Jews. I thought about my heritage and the

trials of my fore-fathers. I tried to swim in the salty Dead Sea but I fell down on the jagged rocks.

Pat insisted I try to ride on a camel. She said my pop had done so when he toured Israel. So I took a short camel ride that frightened me. The poor thing had trouble standing and related that trouble to me.

We walked the Via Dolorosa, the same road that Jesus walked on the way to his crucifixion. We saw the wall that the Jews had erected in Jerusalem to "keep out" the modern day, unwanted Arabs.

We drove through an Israeli "checkpoint" from Bethlehem, in Palestine, into Jewish controlled territory. Two teenagers, boy and girl, dressed like combat soldiers, fingers on Uzi guns, stopped us and boarded the bus, asking who we were. The tour guide responded, "Pilgrims from the US."

"Passports!" the Israeli teenagers demanded.

Since I was in the first seat of the first row, I was the first one to have my passport read. The teenage girl said, "Cohen?"

I answered, "Yes!"

"Jewish?" she again asked.

I again answered, "Yes!"

She quickly said, "Pass the whole bus!"

Sometimes it pays to be Jewish.

We visited the Wailing Wall, now called the Western Wall

of Jerusalem. It is the holiest of Jewish sights in the world today. I was invited to read the famous passage from Deuteronomy in the Bible to my other pilgrims. I donned my yarmulke (a Jewish skullcap) and I wore my Tallus, the Jewish prayer shawl given to me by my parents for my Bar Mitzvah, over sixty years ago. I read, "Schmaha Yisroel, Adonoi Elihanu, Adonoi echad!" Almost shouting, I said, "Hear O' Israel, the Lord is my God, the Lord is One!" I cried.

Father Chris asked if he could accompany me and touch the Wall. I agreed but said he should put the Cross of Christ out of sight and he should wear a yarmulke. Surrounded by only men, (women were secondary to men, according to old Hebrew philosophy), we both approached the Wall. Both of us inserted a wish or prayer in cracks in the wall previously prepared. Needless to say, mine was for Pat's health.

I made the sign of the Cross on my chest. Father Chris leaned over to me and whispered, "We don't do that here." "Oh," I answered. I had been to so many Catholic Masses those two weeks, I forgot where I was. The Christians had gotten to me.

Overlooking Jerusalem. I am on the far right, in the second row, the outcast Jew!

Our pilgrimage was exciting, interesting and very illuminating. Being proselytized was my original concern but I was still glad to be a Jew. Those kind Catholic pilgrims called me a "Son of Abraham" and asked me to bless them and the Jewish jewelry they purchased!

Our Trip to Alaska

In September 2005, my cancer-filled Pat and I took a ten-day cruise to Alaska. It was the first time either of us had been to Alaska and we thoroughly enjoyed it. Everyone said we would, and many had cruised there more than once.

Everyday we were cruising, Pat and I attended Catholic Mass. It was a healing experience for Pat and an hour of nodding off and/or daydreaming of "nuggets" for my newspaper column.

A retired Maryknoll Missionary Priest, Father Jack King, declared that he was a "Jack and a King without a Queen," and I added he was also an "Ace" because of his humor and common sense. More than once in his homilies he spoke to me as a proud Jew.

Father King told us several times that Catholics shouldn't read prayers from their Missals because these are the words of someone else. Instead, we should all, Jews and Catholics alike, go to the outside deck,

We were celebrating our 39th anniversary; the waiter brought us a special cake

lean over the railing and speak to God, in our own words as if God and/or Jesus was at the railing with us. It was certainly a different type of sermon.

After every Mass, Father King collected money for the natives in Costa Rica. I have been to Masses where the hosts were forgotten but never the collection basket. Jesus must have been with all of us because Pat is still holding out against her cancer.

Though I may have claimed to be bored, I enjoyed each Mass at 5:00PM. When over, it was dinnertime that I enjoyed even more.

There was a funny incident on the trip in Sitka, Alaska. While there, Pat and I wanted a local newspaper so I went into a drug store and asked the young lady, slow and pedantically, "Do-you-speak-English?"

She answered, "Occasionally."

I had forgotten that Alaska was in the United States! We both laughed.

And Finally...

CHAPTER TWENTY-ONE

Last year, a good friend of mine lost his wife to heart disease. He had her cremated and never had a formal funeral for those who loved her.

So, a neighbor friend decided to have a little memorial gathering in his garden so that we could all say goodbye to a fine lady. Since the deceased woman and her husband were baptized as Catholics, but had not attended any church for over forty years, the husband asked me (a Jew, of all people) to see if I could get a Catholic priest to say a few words at the memorial gathering. The only reason I could fathom for my being asked was that he knew Pat and I were friendly with all the priests at our local Sts. Simon and Jude Parrish.

I went to see Father Christian Mondor, my good friend from the pilgrimage to Israel earlier that year. I explained to him that this couple had not attended church for a long while, but the husband wondered if he would mind conducting an appropriate religious service in the neighbor's garden. Of course, Father Chris said yes. I thanked him and said that Pat and I would pick him up the next day.

The next day, we picked up Father Chris and took him to the house. Father Chris said a few passages from his Missal and led us in a prayer and a song. Then Father asked to speak, privately, to the bereaved husband. Father Chris had a short conversation with my friend and then Pat and I took him back to the parish priests' home. When I asked him about his short conversation with the husband, Father responded, "I asked him if he would like to talk to me in private back at the Church at his convenience. He said he would let me know."

Several months later, my friend said that he had spoken to Father Christian several times, that he had "heard his confession," given him some sort of "benediction" and welcomed him back into the Catholic faith.

You may not understand this but I feel this is, and will remain, my greatest contribution to my friend and to the Catholic Church. And I feel that God has blessed me as well.

Post Script

You think it's not easy being a Jew?

Try being the daughter of a Jew *and* a Catholic.

Talk about guilt? The only thing worse than Catholic guilt is Jewish guilt.

My parents wanted me to write a conclusion for my father's book. I told them I wasn't a writer and didn't want to do it…but you see that I succumbed to the guilt and wrote it anyway.

The stories you read in this book are all nearly true. If you know my father, then you know how he can exaggerate at times. Still, these stories I have heard many times, from him and from other family members, so that we all now believe them to be fact. It makes me wonder, though, if there's any truth to the stories that are missing from the book. Like the one about the day the furnace was broken in his elementary school, and he broke a wooden desk and lit it on fire—*in the classroom*—to heat the room. Or the one where he was working for the FBI and attended communist party meetings to secretly report their activities. During one of the meetings, the leader announced that there was a spy in the room and my dad flatly denied it. He had to leave town so as not to be shot—which supposedly was the real reason he moved to California in 1963.

In any case, it's nice to have these stories written down for everyone to read. It allows so many more people to know who my father is and what his life was like. As he would always say, "Aren't you glad you know me? Don't you wish everyone did?"

—*Susan Cohen Locke*